## GROWING UP

# My New Brother or Sister

# or Sister

Charlotte Guillain

Raintree

**www.raintreepublishers.co.uk**
Visit our website to find out
more information about
Raintree books.

**To order:**
☎ Phone 0845 6044371
🖨 Fax +44 (0) 1865 312263
💻 Email myorders@raintreepublishers.co.uk

Customers from outside the UK please telephone +44 1865 312262

Raintree is an imprint of Capstone Global Library Limited, a company incorporated in England and Wales having its registered office at 7 Pilgrim Street, London, EC4V 6LB – Registered company number: 6695582

Text © Capstone Global Library Limited 2011
First published in hardback in 2011
First published in paperback in 2012
The moral rights of the proprietor have been asserted.

Edited by Dan Nunn, Rebecca Rissman, and Sian Smith
Designed by Joanna Hinton-Malivoire
Picture research by Elizabeth Alexander
Originated by Capstone Global Library Ltd
Printed and bound in China by Leo Paper Products Ltd

ISBN 978 1 406 22016 2 (hardback)
15 14 13 12 11
10 9 8 7 6 5 4 3 2 1

ISBN 978 1 406 22336 1 (paperback)
16 15 14 13 12 11
10 9 8 7 6 5 4 3 2 1

**British Library Cataloguing in Publication Data**
Guillain, Charlotte.
My new brother or sister. – (Growing up)
1. Brothers and sisters–Pictorial works–Juvenile literature.
I. Title II. Series
306.8'75-dc22

**Acknowledgements**
We would like to thank the following for permission to reproduce photographs: Alamy pp. 8 (© Glow Wellness RM 97), 12, 23 glossary nappy (© Bubbles Photolibrary), 18 (© Picture Press); © Capstone Publishers pp. 17, 19 (Karon Dubke); Corbis p. 11 (© David P. Hall); Getty Images pp. 4, 23 glossary pregnant (Lori Adamski Peek/Workbook Stock), 5 (Michael Wildsmith/Taxi), 13 (Andersen Ross/Stockbyte), 20 (Tony Anderson/Taxi); iStockphoto pp. 10 (© zhang bo), 14 (© jo unruh), 22 bottom middle (© Jenny Swanson); Photolibrary pp. 6, 23 glossary hospital (Corbis), 7 (Image Source), 9, 23 glossary incubator (Upitis Alvis/Imagestate), 16 (Nicole Hill/Rubberball), 21, glossary jealous (Picture Partners/age footstock); Shutterstock pp. 15 (© Monkey Business Images), 22 top left (© jcpjr), 22 top middle (© Lim Yong Hian), 22 top right (© Myotis), 22 bottom left (© Stephen Coburn), 22 bottom right (© Margo Harrison).

Front cover photograph of a girl holding a baby reproduced with permission of Photolibrary (Clarissa Leahy). Back cover photograph of baby clothes reproduced with permission of © Capstone Publishers (Karon Dubke), and a bath reproduced with permission of iStockphoto (© jo unruh).

Every effort has been made to contact copyright holders of material reproduced in this book. Any omissions will be rectified in subsequent printings if notice is given to the publisher.

# Contents

Some words are shown in bold, **like this**.
You can find them in the glossary on page 23.

# What happens before a new baby arrives?

When your family is expecting a new baby, your mum will be **pregnant**.

Her tummy will get bigger and she may be more tired than normal.

Your family will need to get ready for the new baby.

They will find your old baby things and maybe buy some new things.

# What happens when the baby is born?

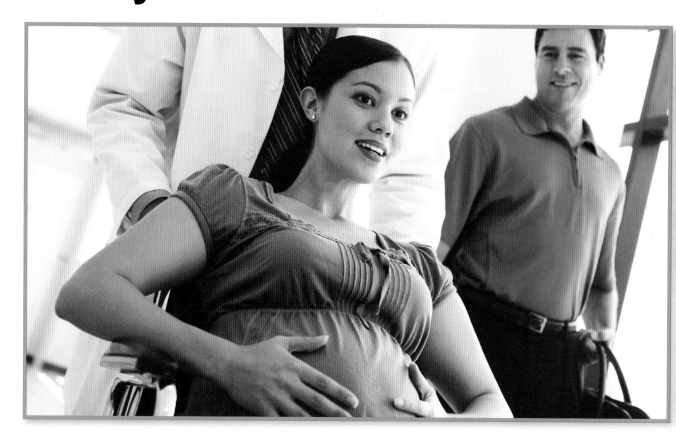

Your mum will probably go to **hospital** to have the baby.

She may have to leave quite suddenly or quickly.

You might go to stay with relatives or friends while your mum is in hospital.

You might miss your mum, but there is no need to feel scared or worried.

# When will I meet my new brother or sister?

You might visit your mum and the baby in **hospital**.

Or you might meet your brother or sister when your mum brings him or her home.

incubator

Some babies have to stay in hospital for a while so the doctors can look after them.

Some babies stay in an **incubator** until they are strong enough to go home.

# What are new babies like?

New babies spend a lot of time sleeping.

They can't sit up or stand until they are much older.

New babies cry and need your mum or dad a lot of the time.

You need to be very gentle with a new brother or sister.

# What do new babies need?

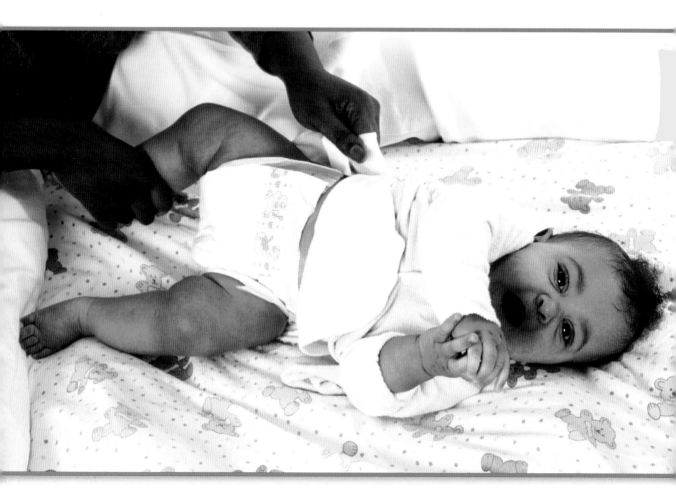

Babies need **nappies** because they can't use the toilet yet.

They also need a special car seat to keep them safe in the car.

New babies can drink milk many times
during the day and night.

They also need lots of sleep in the
daytime and at night.

# Why does the baby need my parents?

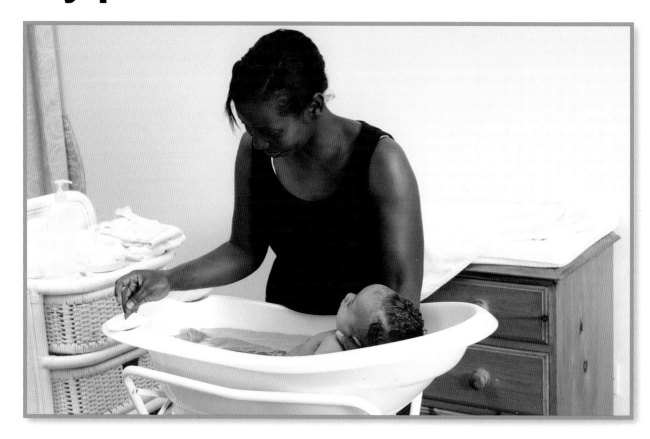

Your mum or dad has to feed, wash, and change the baby many times a day.

They also need to cuddle the baby when he or she cries.

Your mum or dad will be sorry they can't spend more time with you.

You can try to do things together when the baby sleeps.

# Can I help look after the new baby?

Your mum or dad might not want you to pick up the baby.

If the baby is crying you could make them laugh by talking or singing to them.

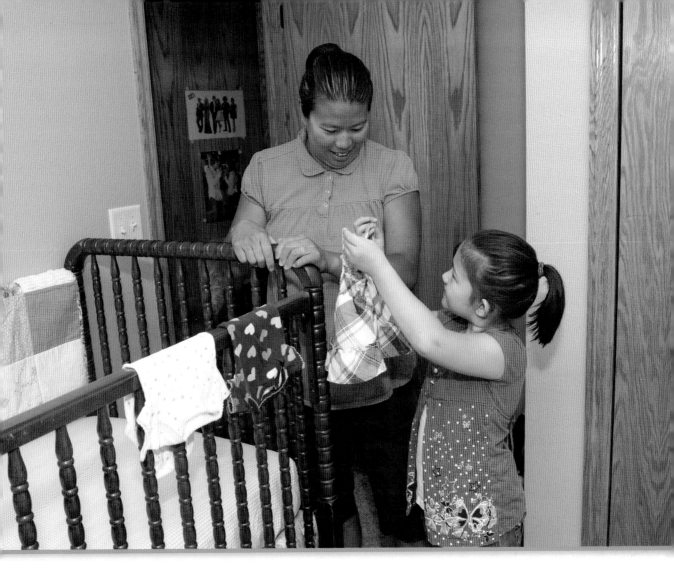

You can bring things that your mum or dad needs when they feed or change the baby.

You might be able to help choose what the baby is going to wear.

# Can the baby play with me?

A new baby won't be able to play with you until he or she is older.

When they are little you can show them toys and books.

When they start crawling they may want
to play with your toys.

You could put your special things away
on a shelf.

# How does the baby make my family feel?

Your parents will feel very happy but they will also be very tired.

They might get cross more than usual because they are so tired.

You might feel **jealous** of the baby for taking up so much of your parents' time.

You might feel excited and proud to have a new brother or sister.

# Baby equipment

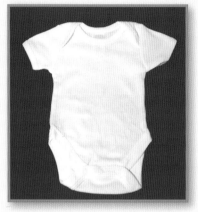

clothes

bottle

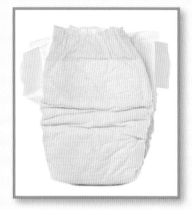

nappy

cot

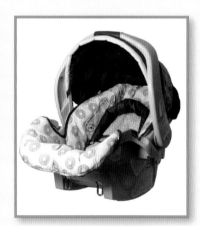

car seat

high chair

# Picture glossary

 **hospital** place where sick people are made better and many women have babies

 **incubator** place that keeps new babies at the right temperature

 **jealous** when you feel bad because you want something somebody else has got

 **nappy** towel or special pants worn by a baby because they can't use the toilet

 **pregnant** expecting a baby

# Find out more

## Books

*Sophie and the New Baby*, Catherine and Laurence Anholt (Orchard, 2004)

*The New Baby*, Anna Civardi and Stephen Cartwright (Usborne, 2005)

*There's a House Inside My Mummy*, Giles Andreae and Vanessa Cabban (Orchard, 2002)

*Waiting for Baby*, Rachel Fuller (Child's Play, 2009)

## Websites

Find out more about welcoming a new baby into the family at:
http://kidshealth.org/kid/feeling/home_family/new_baby.html

## Index